MW01628313

What is Death?

Written by Margaret Wieland

Illustrated by Caleb Salisbury

Author's note

This is a book to be *read to* (with) children, not just given to them.

In recent years I have been blessed to have the company of a little one who has grown up asking questions. Some I could answer easily—others took a bit more thought—and still others caused me to find simpler ways of explaining some of the most profound truths, which always come back to the biggest issue of them all—God and the way His Word intersects with our lives and all of reality. Whilst I think (like all grandparents, I suppose) that she is a special child, I know that her questions are not unique. The questions—and their answers—are told in simple language, with added explanations for the reader where they might be useful.

I can think of no better way for a little child to learn the realities of the universe than on the lap of a loving adult. It is my prayer that adults and children will treasure the time shared together, as we did, while laying a solid biblical foundation in young minds.

Published and distributed by

www.creationbookpublishers.com

Author's Dedication

To my darling 'granddaughter' Mary-Beth: you have so enriched my life that it would be wrong not to share some of our experiences together with others.

www.pleasenana.com

Copyright © 2020 Creation Book Publishers. All rights reserved. No part of this book may be reproduced in any manner whatsoever without written permission of the publisher, except in the case of brief quotations in articles and reviews.

For information on creation/evolution issues and materials for all ages, visit:

CREATION.com

ISBN: 9781921643194
First printing 2010
Second printing 2013
Third printing 2017
Fourth printing 2020

Hi—I'm Bilby, a small, cute and cuddly looking animal that lives in Australia. I'm Nana's friend, and I can be yours too—look for me on every double-page spread.

[1] A bilby is a small cute Australian animal (for more information see p.25).

About the Author:

Margaret Wieland is the eldest of seven children, a Christian for well over 50 years, a mother, grandmother and great grandmother who (though widely traveled) has lived in Australia all her life. She is fond of telling anyone who listens that "these later years are the best time of life, particularly if you can share that life with young children. They make you look at familiar things with fresh eyes and bring a newness of life to old beliefs. There are no greater treasures we can leave a child (related or not) than our unconditional love, our unhurried time, a love for God and His Word, and as many shared experiences as possible. It's the closest thing to the 'Fountain of Youth' you will ever find."

About the Illustrator:

Caleb Salisbury is a professional illustrator with an extensive background in game development and graphic design. He grew up in Africa and now lives in Brisbane (Australia), where he enjoys creating entertaining stories featuring whimsical characters and visually rich environments for all ages. He currently works for *Creation Ministries International.*

He says he also drinks far too much coffee.

A little girl stands quiet and still,
Her mind is all a-muddle:
Why does the pretty bird that flew
Lie lifeless in the puddle? [2]
A gentle breeze stirs one small wing;
Bright feathers now just lie.
She knows it's dead and will not move;
I hear a tiny sigh. [3]

It is so hard to understand,
Though I could see her try.
She looks at me, the question comes,
"Why, Nana, why'd he die?"
"Oh, I don't know—it's hard to say;
Perhaps he had a fright.
Or maybe he was very sick
But tried for one more flight."

I sat her on the ground with me,
The day was near its end;
And while we settled into place
I spoke to my small friend.
"Remember when your grandma died
And you were crying too?
Mum said she'd died and gone to Heav'n,
Far, far away from you." [4]

"You'd spent a lot of time with her;
That made you both feel glad.
Her death would bring an end to this
And all the fun you'd had." [5]
We gazed down on that little bird;
I heard her catch her breath.
The words came slow but so distinct,
"Please, Nana, what is death?"

I looked into those big brown eyes,
So fixed upon my face;
There may not be a better time
Or any better place.
"There was a world long years ago, [6]
Where nothing ever died;
No-one got sick or hurt themselves,
And no-one ever cried." [7]

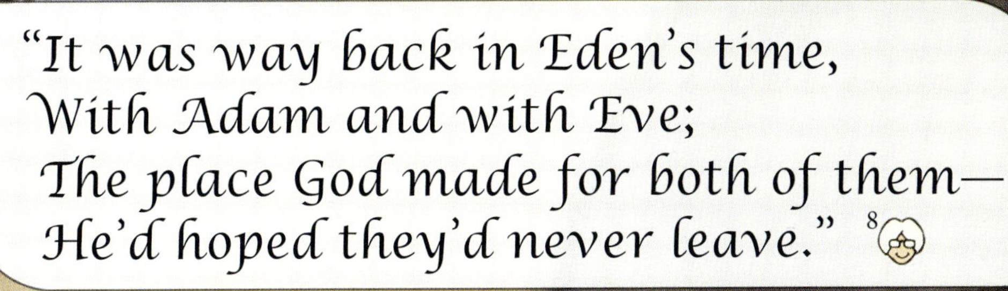

"It was way back in Eden's time,
With Adam and with Eve;
The place God made for both of them—
He'd hoped they'd never leave." [8]

"These two were very happy there
In that amazing place;
And daily God would meet with them,
And they'd talk face to face."

"Adam was warned by God before,
About a certain tree;
'Don't eat of this', God clearly said,
'You'll die most certainly'." [9]
GOD
Don't eat the fruit
"And Adam had a word with Eve,
When she became his wife:
'Don't ever eat fruit from this tree,
Or we will lose our life.'"

'But, lurking just a short way off,
Another creature hid—
Perhaps behind that very tree
Whose fruit God did forbid." [10]

"This being was created too,
But lost his lofty place;
He was so jealous as he thought
(a sly look on his face):" [11]

"'I wonder, could I get these two
To help themselves to that?
Hmmm, Adam maybe no, not him.'
Then saw where Eve had sat." 12
"'She's thinking still of that nice fruit,
Imagining for sure
How very special it would taste,
And wanting, more and more—'" 13

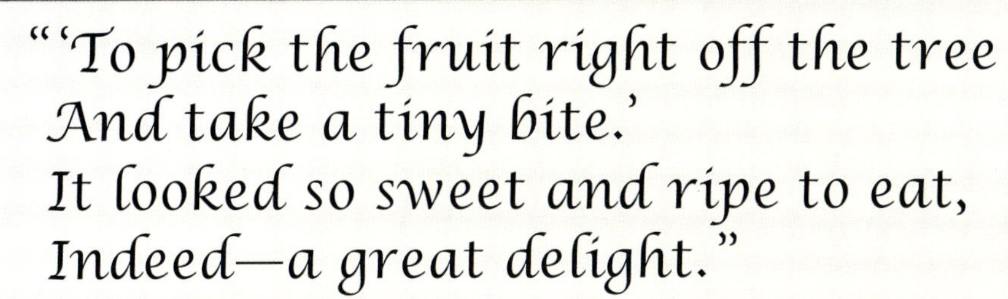

“‘To pick the fruit right off the tree
And take a tiny bite.’
It looked so sweet and ripe to eat,
Indeed—a great delight.”

“This creature quietly closer crept
And headed straight for Eve;
He made himself real charming as
He set out to deceive.”

"'Did God really say, "Don't eat"?',
That didn't sound quite right.
By getting her to doubt God's Word,
'Twas then she took a bite." [14]
"It's fairly certain Adam saw
And overheard the two;
It seems to me, Eve didn't ask
Her husband what to do." [15]

"The Bible's clear that when Eve bit,
The world still looked the same—
So had God set a test for them?
Or was it just a game?"
"When Adam saw the sampled fruit
That Eve held in her hand,
He thought of all he'd heard God say,
When He that fruit had banned."

"He loved Eve so, but God had said,
'Eat that and you will die'.
But here she was alive and well;
Was that just one big lie?"
"But, Adam may have worried then,
If true, she'd go away.
And what of him? He'd be alone ...
Such thoughts would cause dismay." 16

“So Adam took a nervous bite,
And instantly he knew:
He wasn’t wearing any clothes,
And Eve was naked too.” [17]

“They heard God coming as He did
At close of every day;
Instead of just approaching Him,
They hid themselves away.”

"God called and called, though He knew well
What dreadful thing they'd done.
The lovely times they had enjoyed
Were gone—and all the fun."

"God asked the man to tell Him why
He'd clearly disobeyed.
At first he tried to blame his wife—
Eve felt, oh, so betrayed."[18]

"But God was having none of that
And made it very clear
That eating fruit of that one tree
Had brought disaster near."
"An animal would have to die,
To cover their bare skins;
God set about to kill a beast,
And that's where death begins." 19

"When that was done and garments made,
God had much more to say.
The Garden was no longer theirs;
They'd leave that very day."
"Because of this all living things
Most certainly will die;
Yes, every kind of animal,
On land, in sea or sky."

"And that means human beings too,
Yes, grandmas, you, and me;
That's why we need to understand
Our early history."
"But don't be sad; God had a way
To make this bad thing right.
Though it would surely take some time
To fix our sorry plight." [20]

"Remember when we spoke before,
Of God, the three-in-one?
The One who came to rescue us
Was Jesus Christ the Son."
"And by His life and through His death,
And rising from it too,
God showed that death is not 'the end',
And all He said was true."

"And you and I and everyone,
Can live again if we
Believe and put our trust in Him,
And claim His love—it's free."
We gently took the little bird,
To bury properly.
In death, he gave a glimpse of life,
And how it's meant to be.

I'm very thankful to that bird,
Though he will never know
God used him in a special way,
To help a small child grow.

..: Nana Notes :..

1 The little 'bilby' character is a native of Australia and a member of the bandicoot family of marsupials. The bilby is about the size of a rabbit. It lives mostly in dry areas of Australia, where it has become endangered, probably due to feral cats and foxes. A shy creature, it comes out at night when things are cooler; during the heat of the day it lives in one of several spiral burrows it has dug to escape things that want to eat it (it's a fallen world!). It sometimes eats other (smaller) furry animals, too, but mostly it eats insects, grubs, seeds, and fruit. Like other marsupials, it has a pouch to raise its young. But its pouch is designed to point backwards, not forwards like a kangaroo's, to avoid it getting filled up with dirt as the bilby burrows.

Bilby was chosen because of his big, hairless ears, which give him very acute hearing—and hearing is very important when someone is reading a story to a child. Not only for the child of course, but also for the reader. Children will ask the most convoluted questions, and we must listen very hard to not only what is being said but to what they actually *mean*, so that we can provide the answers they are genuinely seeking. The Bible says that faith comes by hearing, and hearing by the Word of God (Romans 10:17)—which includes proclaiming, expounding and explaining ('preaching') its truths.

A soft toy bilby has been to the Top of the World!! In May 1997, Tashi Tenzing—grandson of Tenzing Norgay, one of the two men who first conquered Mount Everest—reached the summit himself. The following extract is from a book written by Tashi and his wife Judy:

> *"On the very top of my pack I had attached a small, fluffy toy bilby, which is a highly endangered Australian marsupial. My son had asked me to carry it and it also symbolised my heartfelt wish to conserve the wild places and creatures of this amazing planet."*

Tenzing Norgay and the Sherpas of Everest, by Judy and Tashi Tenzing 2001

More on bilbies: members.optusnet.com.au/bilbies/About_Bilbies.htm.

[2]  This is a true story. A little bird died almost at our feet. This event led to an opportunity to discuss, only briefly at the time, the presence of death in the midst of life. Don't be afraid to talk about this subject with children when they ask—many will have had some acquaintance with death already, some even from a very early age.

---

[3]  You may well be asked, "Do animals go to Heaven when they die?" You will find a great deal of speculation on the internet on this subject, much of it unfortunately 'wishful thinking'. Even for 'soulish' animals (*nephesh chayyah*) the Bible makes it plain that there is a difference between the 'spirit' of an animal and that of a person (Ecclesiastes 3:21). People were created in God's image (Genesis 1:26–27)—animals were not. A good article on this subject, written by an animal lover who wants to promote God's word, is available at creation.com/animal-souls. See also, "Can bunny rabbits be saved? Will there be animals in the new Creation?" (creation.com/bunny)

---

[4]  It did help that my little friend had experienced the death of her (real, paternal) grandmother just a few months earlier and we had already discussed the topic at some length. Of course, when it comes to people, especially loved ones, the issue of 'where are they now' is part of it. It's normally accepted that one tells young children that the deceased has 'gone to Heaven'—and even most adults think in these terms. The starker reality of what the Bible has to say on anyone's ultimate destination can be put off for a later date, but each child is different, and some are ready earlier than others to face up to this. But the Bible is very clear: "And as it is appointed unto men once to die, but after this the judgment." (Hebrews 9:27)

[5] In our super-sensitive society, we use euphemisms to cover our own embarrassment when the harsh facts of life in this fallen world are too hard to contemplate. In place of 'death' we substitute 'gone to sleep', 'passed away', 'resting in peace' etc. As Christians, we know that death has been overcome through Christ(1 Corinthians 15:47–57), and it should hold no further fears for us. It is that concept and attitude we need to convey to our children.

---

[6] Rather than avoiding words like *long ago* in case they might suggest that creation is millions of years old, I would encourage parents to consider that the 6,000 or so years for the straightforward biblical moment of creation is really a very long time ago. We've been conditioned otherwise mostly because of the way our evolutionized culture promotes the concept of 'millions of years'. The Bible writers, and great minds of the past, including scientists like Sir Isaac Newton, had no difficulty using words like *ancient* to describe things like mountains (e.g., Deuteronomy 33:15). Yet they knew from Scripture that nothing was more than about six thousand years old. By stating clearly that people were there from the beginning of creation (Mark 10:6 and elsewhere), Jesus Himself left no room for eons of time before Adam. Equally, the fossils, with their record of death, disease and suffering, were not laid down millions of years before sin ruined a perfect world. They are, instead, the record of God's (post-Adam) judgment on sin by way of the massive global flood catastrophe described in three whole chapters of Genesis. For more see creation.com/the-earth-how-old-does-it-look; see also creation.com/age-of-the-earth for a long list of evidences of recent creation.

7 Presumably you've already read *Please, Nana ... Who is God?* Referring back to that book would be a good thing to do now. See creation.com/creation-for-kids for some great explanations of life in that special garden. CMI also has an excellent children's book *Days 1–7* (among other items) available at creation.com/store.

---

8 Children usually have very active imaginations and have little difficulty picturing scenes in their own minds. The artist has cleverly used this little one's imaginings to bring to life a scene we find very difficult to illustrate any other way—keeping to the truth of Scripture but avoiding controversy over, for example, how to depict our first parents in a book for children. .

---

9 The Bible has two accounts of the creation story—in Genesis 1 and 2. See creation.com/genesis-questions-and-answers if people try to tell you about so-called 'contradictions' in Genesis.

---

10 Just as we cannot possibly identify the forbidden 'fruit', which was not from any tree that exists today, neither can we be totally certain as to the physical form this 'serpent' took. It may be that it was very beautiful, and it was certainly quite beguiling. Eve would have had no reason to cringe from it in fear as we might today upon seeing a snake. Every single thing in Eve's young experience was beautiful and good and she had no concept of evil in any shape or form. And this particular 'serpent' could also speak. Adam could, Eve could, and God certainly did—so it would have been an understandable assumption on Eve's part that this creature was of some importance, too, in the scheme of things.

11 Was this 'being' just another creature that God had created on Day Five? Yes—and no—certainly the 'serpent' was in animal form, but the fact that it could speak in words clearly understood by Eve makes it very different from every other animal in existence at that time. The Bible states clearly that God made all things in heaven and earth in those six days (Exodus 20:11), so even the angels had to be created during that time (Colossians 1:16)—and it is likely that they were created in the first part of Day 1, just before the earth (Job 38: 4 & 7). These created angels all remained true to their Creator right up to the very end of Day 6 of the Creation Week, when God pronounced everything He had made 'very good'. But the Bible also indicates that somewhere after that point and before the temptation of Eve, there was a rebellion in Heaven led by a being high in the angelic hierarchy, whom we now call the devil or Satan. He is described in glowing terms (Ezekiel 28:11–19). He may well have been an amazingly beautiful being. Before Eve and then Adam made the choice to go against God, so had this 'anointed cherub' who, as it appears, also encouraged no less than a third of the hosts of angels to join with him in this mutiny (Revelation 12:4). So, yes, this serpent was a real animal but Satan gave him voice (Revelation 12:9). For more, see creation.com/who-was-the-serpent.

---

12 This has been perhaps the hardest of all the points to cover, for the following reasons. Genesis 2 explains only that God told Adam not to eat the fruit of "the tree of the knowledge of good and evil" (Genesis 2:16–17). Genesis 3:2–3 makes it clear that Adam MUST have passed on to Eve the prohibition regarding eating of one specific tree, just as he must surely have shown that tree to her. Whether Eve was near that tree, sitting down or standing up, hankering after the fruit or not, when and where the serpent accosted her, we can only surmise. That she was open to discussion about what God had said, and the fact that Eve even elaborated on God's own words (verse 3), makes it clear that she was wavering in her own resolve already—or at the very least trying to shore it up. I have used a little poetic license here to illustrate the important aspect of temptation, and how easy it was for the serpent to cajole Eve into disobedience. An excellent article on Eve's temptation, and a profound explanation of the importance of her thoughts, words and actions can be seen at creation.com/strategy-of-the-devil.

13 How like Eve we all are. Forbid something (especially when it looks so tempting) and resisting the temptation becomes nigh intolerable. What mom or grandma has not put a tray of freshly baked cookies on the counter and uttered these same words—"Don't touch." Does it work? Hmm ... it's hard to resist the lure of a fresh-baked cookie, and what child is not prepared to risk even a small burn to taste one sooner rather than later? Curiosity is a great character trait, but its exercise has to be tempered with knowledge handed down from experience. God knew 'curiosity' would be a mainstay of the human race, but he also knew it would need direction from One who had their very best interests at heart. Satan, or the Serpent, had only *his* best interests at heart.

---

14 Hover around it, touch it, take it, eat it—the lure of temptation! Haven't we all been guilty of doing just that—and lived to regret it later? Back to our cookies on the bench—or that chocolate in the fridge—or the toy your friend just received for their birthday that you just had to have a play with. Illustrations are everywhere. Our daily papers have regular accounts of people responding in just that way—and having to face the consequences of their actions. The lesson? Don't hang around things that are tempting. Move away. Put them out of sight and out of mind. Did Eve do that? No. Did Satan know he had a chance with Eve because of that? Most certainly.

---

15 

Genesis 3:6—Adam seems to have been nearby yet did not try to deter Eve from eating the fruit. He knew better and should have stopped her. What adult has not regretted taking their eyes off one in their care (as Eve was in Adam's) for an instant and then having to rescue that child from a dangerous situation?

16  Eve sampled the fruit—and nothing seemed to happen. How often are we led, as children and adults, to feel secure in doing something wrong when we have seen others get away with it? Adam was very likely in turmoil. He had heard what God said and he had believed Him, but here was Eve alive and well and nothing had changed—yet. We can well imagine that doubt crept in. And before long, Adam found himself joining Eve in this trespass against God.

---

17  The little illustration says it all. Instantly, Adam and Eve both knew that the life they had known was over. Everything had changed. They were in deep, deep trouble. They were estranged from each other, estranged from this beautiful new world and estranged from God—Genesis 3:7–8.

---

18  Oh, yes, we all know how to put the blame on someone else. Adam blamed Eve and, because God had given Eve to him, he tried to transfer some of that blame to God Himself—Genesis 3:12. Hapless Eve blamed the serpent. But God places the responsibility firmly at the feet of Adam.

For further clarification of this difficult subject, please read Romans 5:12–19 and creation.com/could-adam-have-appealed-the-verdict.

---

19  And so death enters this idyllic world. An animal (or several) would have to die—a perfectly innocent, harmless animal—to provide covering for these two. The Hebrew word translated 'atonement' is כפר (*kaphar*), which means 'cover'. That first blood sacrifice may have even been a lamb, as a forerunner of the sinless, perfect Lamb of God, Jesus Christ, who atoned for the sin of all who would put their trust in Him, once for all time. The Garden of Eden was no longer their 'home', and the world was going to be a very harsh place indeed. It's worth reading creation.com/the-tree-of-life-garden-of-eden for a serious look at the main reason Adam and Eve had to leave the Garden.

20 It's easy to see why these events in the Garden are crucial to understanding the Christian gospel. Sin and death entered this world through (the first) Adam, and these two 'enemies' were dealt a mortal blow through the death and resurrection of Christ (whom the Bible calls "the last Adam"—see creation.com/first-adam-last-adam). For more answers about this whole issue of death coming via the Fall (for all *nephesh* life, not just people), creation.com/death-questions leads to a whole bunch of great articles.

Acknowledgment

Before I started on this venture, I believed that writing books for children would be less difficult than writing for adults. "Iron sharpens iron" indeed (Proverbs 27:17) and this book is as useful as it was meant to be because a number of gifted, mature Christians made invaluable contributions. It is hard to name them all; some simply gave encouragement, others pointed out where either words or drawings needed adjustment in order to remain true to the Word of God, while the editorial skills of quite a few were vital. To them, and to those who had already written much on this subject and whose work I have unashamedly utilized—my heartfelt thanks. And it goes without saying, perhaps, that without Caleb's magnificent drawings, these simple words would not have sprung so profoundly to life.